SPIRIT OF THE DRAGON

Chloe E. Gore

In a small Chinese town surrounded by pagodas and colorful lanterns, siblings named Wei and Fang live.

The Chinese New Year always fills them with excitement and joy. This year, the celebration is going to be special as it marks the Year of the Dragon.

For the first time, their parents involve the children in joint activities, ensuring that the preparations will be unforgettable.

The first task on their list is to clean the house. Tradition holds that a clean home on Chinese New Year brings good luck and prosperity for the entire year.

The children work together, cleaning every corner, removing dust from furnitures, and restoring luster to decorations.

Then the preparation of festive dishes begins.

The siblings decide to help their parents prepare traditional Chinese dishes such as: Jiǎozi, Yú, and Nian Gao.

Wei assists in cooking, while Fang helps by cutting vegetables and mixing sauces.

In the meantime, they also start decorating the house with red lanterns and colorful banners with wishes for prosperity.

The red color is particularly important, considered the color of happiness and protection against evil spirits.

The siblings also create decorative symbols from paper, such as dragons and flowers, to add a magical touch to their home.

When the Spring Festival begins, children dress in traditional Chinese attire.

Wei wears Tangzhuang with dragon embroidery, while Fang wears a beautiful silk Qipao.

Together with their parents, they go to the temple to pray for good fortune, health, and prosperity in the coming year.

Upon returning home they enjoy a special dinner with many delicious Chinese dishes.

Dumplings shaped like coins are on the table for good luck.

A sticky rice cake, called Nian Gao, symbolizes a happy and successful new year.

A fish (pronounced as 'yu' in Chinese) is a sign of prosperity.

The entire family enjoys these delicious dishes and laughs together, making the celebration extra special!

After the meal, it is time for the traditional handing out of red envelopes containing money.

Wei and Fang receive them from their parents, grandparents, and relatives, symbolizing blessings and a good start to the new year.

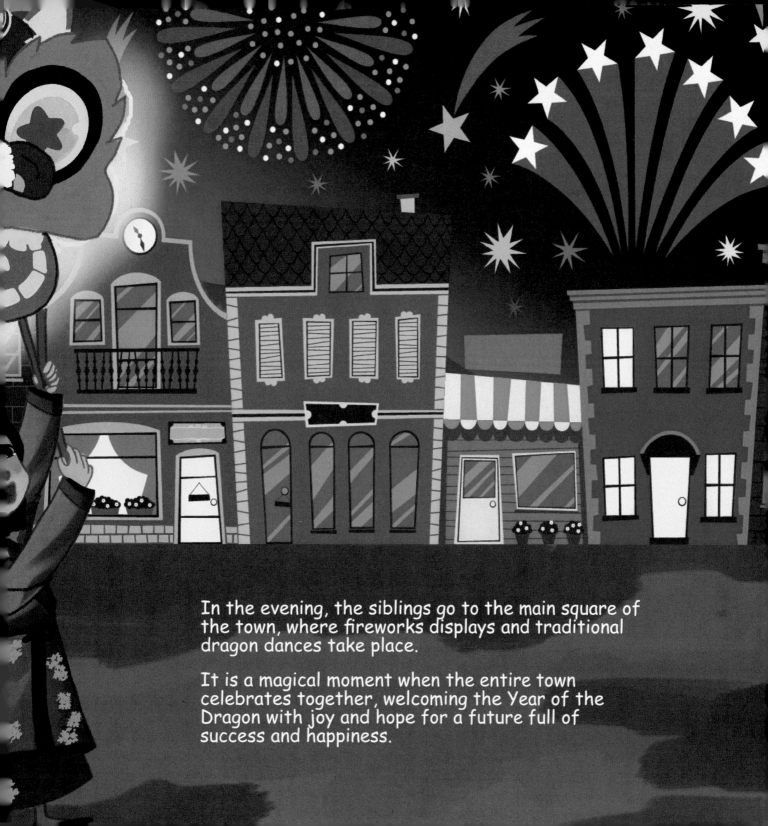

In the evening, the siblings go to the main square of the town, where fireworks displays and traditional dragon dances take place.

It is a magical moment when the entire town celebrates together, welcoming the Year of the Dragon with joy and hope for a future full of success and happiness.

Wei and Fang, with smiles on their faces, return home, knowing that their efforts in preparing for the Chinese New Year have borne fruit.

They know that this special day strengthens family bonds and a sense of community, and the traditions they pass down through generations form the foundation of their Chinese identity.

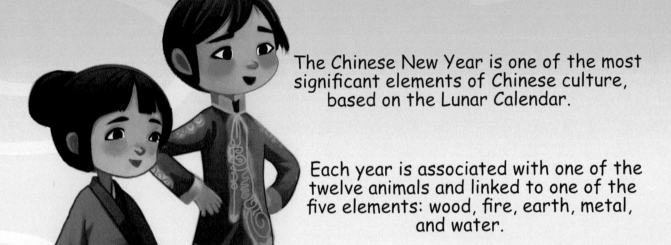

The Chinese New Year is one of the most significant elements of Chinese culture, based on the Lunar Calendar.

Each year is associated with one of the twelve animals and linked to one of the five elements: wood, fire, earth, metal, and water.

In the Chinese zodiac calendar, animals include: rat, ox, tiger, rabbit, dragon, snake, horse, goat, monkey, rooster, dog, and pig. Each child born in a specific year is connected to one of these animals.

Colorful decorations: During the Chinese New Year celebration, traditional colors like red, symbolizing luck, and gold, representing wealth, are used. Red lanterns, ornaments, and banners are popular during this festive occasion.

Customs and traditions: During the Chinese New Year, people follow various customs, such as cleansing their homes to ward off evil spirits and giving children red envelopes with money for good luck.

Fireworks displays: Fireworks shows are popular during the Chinese New Year celebrations in China and other Asian countries. They are considered a way to drive away evil spirits and bring happiness into the new year.

Dragon and lion dances: Colorful dragon and lion parades are organized in many places worldwide. These symbolic creatures dance and move during the parade, bringing joy and happiness.

Made in the USA
Las Vegas, NV
29 January 2024